MARIA NEWHOUSE

Glimmering Moments

Lessons in the Chaos

For the ones who made me a mother—
and the village who held me together.

Contents

Preface

This collection of essays on motherhood started with a nudge—actually, a lot of nudges—from friends online.

"You should write a book," they'd tell me, usually after I posted some long-winded thought about parenting or life.

"About what?" I'd shoot back.

But somewhere in there, I realized it: *I already had a book.* A short book, perhaps, but a book nonetheless. I had written thousands of words scattered across social media posts, voice memos, and half-typed notes on my phone—words about being a parent, a woman, a wife, a professional. Stories I'd been living and collecting for years.

The only thing I didn't have was the time. Or so I told myself. But then, one day, I decided to stop waiting for the perfect moment and just started. I dug through social media posts late at night. I jotted thoughts when I could. I wrote in the margins of everyday life, because I needed to get the stories out of my head—and into the world.

And here it is.

This book doesn't promise answers. It's not a guide or a manual. It's just a collection of moments—messy, tender, chaotic moments—that I wanted to hold onto. Along the way, I started to see the shape of something I hadn't fully noticed in real time: a pattern of letting go, holding on, growing up (again), and learning to trust myself.

It turns out there really are lessons in the chaos. Some of them are loud. Most of them are quiet. All of them are honest.

If these essays offer anything, I hope it's this: that you are already doing more than enough. That you're allowed to grow and grieve and get it wrong. That love, even messy and chaotic, is still more than worthy.

I hope this collection resonates with you. But even if it doesn't—at least I wrote it.

And that, in its own small way, is a kind of a becoming too.

I

The Birth of a Mother

"Sleep at this point is just a concept...something to look forward to investigating in the future." – Amy Poehler

1

To Charlotte Allyn

You were born yesterday at 11:35 a.m., weighing in at 7 pounds 12 ounces and measuring 19.5 inches long. We're a bit biased, but we think you're pretty perfect.

My contractions started Wednesday evening around 5 p.m.—really light at first. I thought maybe it was false labor or Braxton-Hicks, so I tried all the usual things to test it: changed positions, drank water, ate, and moved around. Around 7, I told your dad I'd been having light contractions for a couple of hours (he wasn't thrilled at the delay in sharing the news with him) and we went for a walk. They stuck around through the walk, so we figured this might actually be it.

I knew it could be a long process, so we crawled into bed around 9 p.m. to try to sleep. That didn't last. I overheated and ended up going downstairs around 11. I managed to fall asleep for about two hours and woke up at 1 a.m.—no contractions right away, which made me think it had all fizzled out. But just as I was about to call it a night (so to speak), the next one hit.

They were about eight minutes apart for a little over an hour—and very manageable—and then suddenly they got intense and dropped to five minutes apart by 3:30. That's when I woke your dad.

By then, lying down was no longer an option. Movement helped. The tub helped for about an hour. So did stairs, surprisingly. And toward the end, laboring on the toilet was my favorite—I certainly wasn't expecting that.

Your Nana arrived shortly before we went to the hospital and flew into the bathroom to give me a hug—despite your dad warning her that I wasn't in the mood to be touched (she learned that quickly).

We headed to the hospital around 8:30 a.m. (and sent Nana quickly back to the house for the camera!) with contractions two to three minutes apart. I was a bit disappointed to only be at 7 centimeters upon arrival, but I moved quickly from there to 8, and then to a "stretchy 9." Things were picking up. I was already making "pushy" sounds during contractions.

Truthfully? It was a bit of a mess when we got there. No one had called our midwife when we checked in with the after-hours line, and they hadn't set up the room for a birth—let alone a water birth. So that was fun to navigate.

We tried birthing in the tub, but it relaxed me too much and my contractions got irregular. So we moved to the bed. It wasn't a birthing bed (because that was how things went during your birth), but by then I just needed to work with what I had (and our midwife was, frankly, no help at all).

Digging back into my memory bank, I remembered a video from our birthing class and pulled several positions from it. Ultimately, I found sitting up and pushing to be the most effective—I could feel the contractions more clearly and make use of them. I alternated between sitting upright and squatting on the back of the bed to help you move past my pelvis.

In the end, I pushed for about two hours. There were a couple of hangups—a small lip of cervix you kept getting caught on (not a fun sensation to have that moved out of the way) and then you had some trouble moving (and staying) down the birth canal. But we kept changing positions, rocking and working through it, you and I.

I didn't want anyone to touch me in those last hours, and I know that was hard for your dad and your Nana. But he stayed by my head, holding space, whispering encouragement and she took the camera and documented the moment for me.

And in the end, we had *you*.

Our girl. Our Charlotte Allyn. You changed everything.

Sweet girl, you made me a mom and I will always love you all the numbers and more than the world. Thank you.

Love,
Mama

2

The Truth About the Beginning

I was recently visiting a friend with a newborn and was reminded of the biggest piece of advice I tend to give to expecting parents who genuinely want the real deal.

"Are you sure?" I always ask them, "because you need to be sure."

Here it is: newborns are angry.

They've been evicted from a warm, cozy environment where every need was met before they even knew they had needs. Suddenly, their tiny bodies are bombarding them with unfamiliar signals they don't understand—and neither do we.

Spoiler alert: Will you know what your newborn's cry means? Probably not. And guess what? Neither do they. At least not for the first 4-6 weeks. Buckle up.

There's this romanticized idea that the newborn stage is blissful and magical. But I think those early days are actually the perfect foreshadowing of what motherhood really is: beautiful, yes, but also overwhelming, relentless, and confusing. And yet, we rarely talk about it *honestly*.

We're supposed to cherish those fleeting moments, regardless of the fact that our bodies are torn apart, we're running on fumes, and we're suddenly responsible—not just for healing ourselves—but for keeping a helpless, fragile human alive. And there's no manual for that.

We need to talk more about what it means to become a mother, to become a parent. About how it reshapes every part of your life—your relationship with yourself, your partner, your community, your ambitions. My children have taught me so much about who I am, who I want to be, and who I'm definitely not.

I wouldn't trade them for the world, and at the same time if I'd had a truly honest picture of what parenting would demand of me—physically, emotionally, existentially—I might have made different choices. Or maybe not. But I like to think that I would've at least walked into it all with eyes wide open.

Someone I know recently shared that Seth Rogen—when asked why he doesn't have or want kids—said that parents tell him parenting is glimmering moments of beauty among a sea of pain. I have no idea if it's true, I didn't bother to look it up.

And you know what? It doesn't matter whether he said it or not because that might really be the truth and we don't talk about that enough. Not in the way it deserves to be talked about. We live in a world that makes absolutely everything harder for parents—emotionally, socially, economically. Nothing about the way our systems are constructed makes raising children make sense—and yet, we do it anyway. Every day, we keep going.

Not because we're saints, and not because we're supposed to feel grateful every second—but because love is stubborn, and powerful, and often completely illogical.

And maybe that's enough to begin.

3

Don't Break the Baby

One day, when she was about four weeks old, my husband brought our daughter upstairs to me with a panicked look in his eyes.

"I think," he said, "that I broke the baby."

She was screaming. Inconsolable. Bright red, like a tiny, furious baby planet Mars.

I did the only thing I could think of. I stripped her naked and pressed her bare skin to mine.

And just like that—she quieted. Her breathing slowed. The world reset itself.

That was the moment we realized: the rules weren't fancy. They weren't complicated. But they were weighty.

Don't break the baby.

It became our motto. Our north star. Our family joke.

Now, years later, anyone in our family who watches our kids often end up grading themselves afterward.

"I think I did okay," they'll say. "C+."

"Nobody got hurt. Nobody cried. I didn't break the baby."

That last part? That's what I started to tell every visitor when they asked what the rules were after Charlotte (and each of our children) was born.

Without missing a beat (and still to this day), I'd respond: *"Don't break the baby."*

It always got a laugh. But I meant it. Deep down, I really meant it because in those early days—when I was still bleeding and breastfeeding and barely sleeping—*everything* felt like it could break her. A wrong hold. A skipped nap. The world.

My job, as I understood it, was to protect her. Not just from physical harm, but from anything that could damage her spirit. Anything that might leave a permanent crack. Anything that might turn into the kind of hurt you carry for life.

And honestly? That's a terrifying weight to carry because the truth is that I can't protect her from everything. I can't bubble wrap her heart. I can't make the world kind. I can't promise that nothing will ever hurt her.

But I *can* do my best not to break her. I can show up. I can listen. I can say I'm sorry when I get it wrong and celebrate her fiercely when she gets it right. I can advocate for her and then teach her how to advocate for herself. I can be the soft place she lands when the world feels hard.

And when I inevitably mess up—and I do—I can try again.

Because parenting isn't about perfection. It's about staying in the room. It's about mending what gets frayed. It's about making sure that even if life knocks them around, they know where to find safety, love, and the courage to try again.

So yeah.

Don't break the baby.

But more importantly?

Be someone who shows up and knows how to help them heal.

4

The System Wasn't Built For Us

Eighteen days. That's all I had with my first daughter before I had to return to work full-time.

Eighteen days before the economic reality of having a child slammed into me. At the time, I was working at my alma mater as a graduate assistant, teaching part-time, and attending graduate school full-time. On paper, it probably looked like a terrible time to have a baby—and maybe it was.

But here's the truth: there is no perfect time to have a child. Some circumstances make it easier, yes—but regardless of when it happens, it's hard.

But this? This was brutal.

My first daughter was born ten days late—on the morning I was supposed to be running a volunteer event. I emailed my boss in the early hours to let him know I wouldn't be in, but that message didn't cascade to the rest of the team like I assumed it would. That meant that right up until I was pushing a human into the world, my phone was buzzing with event questions. Eventually, someone realized what was happening and told me to forget everything—they had it covered, and they wished me luck.

There's a lot I could say about the physical toll of that birth, but the bigger lessons came after.

My body was still stitched together. My hormones were chaos. But the bills didn't care about my recovery, and neither did the system. If I didn't go back to my teaching contracts and graduate assistantship, we'd lose the income that helped support our new family of three—not to mention the tuition support that made graduate school possible.

So, I went back. What other choice did I have? (Other than to envy the really civilized countries around the world that provide paid leave to new parents, that is.)

That first day was a full twelve hours. I spent eight hours in my graduate assistant role, including giving a campus tour to some of our new students. We were walking across campus when someone asked, "Why are you walking so slowly?"

I stopped. Right there next to the flagpoles, in that exceedingly echoey part of campus where every word carries, I said, "Because I split myself open two weeks ago giving birth and I'm still stitched together. *Please excuse me if I'd rather not split back open.*"

My voice carried. But you know what? Everyone slowed their roll. Literally.

After my eight-hour shift I had two back-to-back two-hour lectures to teach. "I just had a baby," I told my students that night, by way of introduction, "so please excuse me, but I'm going to sit for this one." That was my one accommodation.

I broke down crying more than once that day. I called my husband to bring me a cushion to sit on and pain killers. My in-laws brought my newborn to campus so I could feed her between shifts—this tiny, perfect human who still felt like a

11

miracle that I was somehow responsible for keeping alive.

That was just the beginning. The first glimpse of what I was starting to understand: that our society talks a good game about supporting families, but when push comes to shove, new mothers are expected to bounce back as if nothing has changed.

And yet, everything had changed. My body. My heart. My understanding of what I was capable of surviving.

But the system? The system wasn't built for us. And that was my first real lesson in how profoundly our society fails families with young children.

5

Finding Space

When I returned to work (again, just eighteen days after giving birth), I needed to pump breast milk every two to three hours. This wasn't optional—it was how I was feeding her.

My supervisor's first suggestion? "You can use the bathroom."

Let me be clear: the suggestion was that I sit on a toilet, balance my equipment, and extract food for my child in a dingy, dirty bathroom stall (without, might I add, electricity to plug my pump in).

I knew better. And thankfully, I had the courage (and the privilege) to escalate the issue to HR. I pointed out that not only was this inappropriate—it was illegal. I was entitled to breaks and a clean, private space. Eventually, those needs were accommodated, but not without complication.

The only place available was the office I shared with other graduate assistants. Regularly, it meant that the space was occupied by up to three other people—of mixed genders.

They made me a window cover. They rearranged their desks and chairs so their backs would face me. They asked what

13

I needed. "Do you want me to leave?" one colleague asked. "Because I'll leave. Or I'll stay and stare at my computer screen until you tell me I'm allowed to look around again. Whatever you need."

I remain forever grateful to these humans who shared that space with me. They never made me feel like a burden. They made me laugh. They made me feel supported. One colleague joked that watching me navigate pregnancy, postpartum, and breastfeeding was probably the best birth control she'd ever experienced.

Truth: If you're on the fence about having kids, just shadow a new mom for a week. It's a real eye opener.

But here's what stays with me:

I had to fight for something that should have been automatic.

I had to advocate for my basic needs during one of the most vulnerable times in my life.

I had to educate other adults about laws that already existed to protect me.

And I was lucky. I had the knowledge to push back. I had supportive colleagues who made space—literally and figuratively. I had a job that couldn't (easily) fire me for making demands.

Not everyone has that. Not everyone knows their rights or has the energy to fight for them when they're running on two hours of sleep and trying to figure out how to keep a tiny human alive.

That's the real tragedy. Not just that the system fails us, but that it fails us during the exact moment when we have the least capacity to fight back.

The accommodations I received shouldn't have been accommodations at all. They should have been the baseline—the absolute minimum of what we offer new parents who are trying to care for their children while contributing to the world.

Instead, I had to learn to advocate for myself in a whole new way. And maybe that's a skill every new mother needs to develop. But, oh, I wish we didn't live in a society where we have to.

6

Learning to Walk: Together

Whoever *they* are—you know, the proverbial "they" who seem to have a quote or a cliché for everything—*they* say that the days are long, but the years are short. I hate how much I agree with that. Because in the blink of an eye, my tiny little baby—always measuring under the 5th percentile for height and weight—wasn't just crawling. She was pulling herself to standing. And then, just like that, she took off walking.

My first child blazed her own path, as first children tend to do. She didn't learn to pull herself up using furniture or people. Instead, she'd put one hand out in front of herself, grab it with the other—like she was shaking her own hand—and use that to balance. For weeks, she just squatted up and down, up and down, right in the middle of our living room.

My mother used to laugh while watching her. She said if she just mimicked Charlotte's movements all day, she'd be the most in-shape nana in the world.

(*And honestly? If you ever have a toddler around, you should try it. I don't think she's wrong.*)

The minute that tiny human figured out how to walk, she took off. And that was both brilliant and terrifying.

I'll never forget being downtown during an art festival. She was exploring everything—touching, observing, laughing, smiling. She wanted to see the world, and I was a nervous wreck. Here was this tiny human, just nine and a half months old and barely fitting into six-month-old clothes, walking around like she owned the place. But she wasn't scared and people? They loved her. They smiled at her confidence and laughed at her wobbling steps.

And that's the thing: those tiny humans of ours aren't afraid until we teach them to be.

Watching them explore is one of the most beautiful gifts of parenting—and one of the hardest. I've often said that parenting is watching my heart walk around outside my body, and I feel it most deeply in moments like that: when they take their first wobbly, wonderful, terrifying steps away from me and into something new. Something they choose. Something they love. Something that begins to shape who they're becoming.

It's a terrifying privilege—stewarding them through these moments, keeping them safe, learning alongside them. We have to give voice to how hard it is to let go, even when we know it's what we're here to do.

Because in the end, isn't that the goal? To raise humans who are capable, confident, and kind enough to carry this messy, beautiful world forward?

But oh, is it hard. And you know what? *They* never said it would be easy.

II

Stretch and Multiply

"Having one child makes you a parent. Having two kids makes you a referee." – *David Frost*

7

To Viviana Renee

We're pretty sure you got things started between 2:30 and 3:00 p.m. yesterday. I was at work when the first contractions hit. They were light and painless at first—so light I wasn't even sure they were real. I didn't say anything to anyone right away. Just your dad and our midwife, Emily.

Not long after that, the contractions picked up. Fast.

I decided to play it safe and head home early. Your dad was at a work event and I figured I had plenty of time, but by the time I pulled out of the parking lot, I knew I didn't. I actually had to pull the car over twice on the drive because the contractions were suddenly that strong. Still, part of me couldn't believe this was really it.

That changed the moment I walked through the door. A fourth contraction hit—hard—and I knew: you were on your way.

Your dad got home not long after I did, and my contractions were already four to five minutes apart. I was on the phone with our midwife, Emily, who was trying to assess whether or not it was really time for her to head over or whether she had time to run home and grab a bite to eat. After listening to me labor for a few minutes, she announced that she would be heading right over. Immediately.

While we waited for her arrival, your dad set up the birth pool in the library. We were supposed to set it up in the living room, but the hose wasn't long enough even though he had measured it in advance just to be sure. We ended up setting the pool up right under a portrait of my dad—your Papa—who we had lost shortly after I found out I was expecting you.

And then guess what happened? I turned on my favorite Pandora station where I was instantly met with a wave of emotion—the very first song that played was "I Loved Her First." It was the song I danced to with him at our wedding. I cannot tell you what that meant to me. Hearing that song in that moment was a gift. I knew he was with us, watching, holding space for your arrival. I cried. But I also felt ready.

By 5 p.m., I was in the birth pool, and it was incredible. Your Nana arrived sometime in the mix of all of this, but I don't know exactly when. My contractions were so strong—every two to three minutes—and I was already dilated to seven. Emily said things were moving quickly, and she was right.

At 6:12, I started to push.

At 6:29, you were here.

I'd love to say it was easy—but it wasn't. You got stuck. Twice. Once because you decided to come out with your arm raised in triumph (absolutely on-brand), and once because your chest was a bit wide. But my body knew what to do. And with a few huge pushes—and Emily's steady hands—you made your way into the world.

My cousin Karina arrived as you made your entrance, scream-

22

ing the moment you arrived, loud and strong. As she snapped photos, you immediately latched like you'd done it a hundred times. The photo she captured in that moment will forever remain one of my favorite images.

And then...you pooped. Twice. According to Emily, it was one of the biggest newborn poops she'd seen in a while. A memorable entrance.

After you were born, we had some complications on my end. But Emily was calm and confident, and I've never felt so well cared for. I trusted her completely. We couldn't have done it without her.

You weighed 8 pounds, 11.5 ounces, and measured 21.25 inches long. And just like that, you were here—and we were never the same.

Viviana Renee. You taught me that a heart can stretch—and that love multiplies. Thank you.

Love,
  Mama

8

Stretch

O ne to Four.
That was the general understanding. The informal agreement.

My husband and I always said we wanted to have at least one kid and probably no more than four. He came from a family of three kids and I am from a family of two.

We almost stopped at one.

We almost stopped at one because it took me a long time after the birth of my first child to even consider having a second. The trauma of her birth was too new and too real, and quite honestly, I didn't have the confidence in myself to think I could do it again.

And if I'm honest with myself? Things just felt perfect the way they were. My daughter had all the attention she needed, there was always one of us to help her, and we'd created this sort of peaceful harmony (as harmoniously as life with a toddler can be, at least). It felt perfect.

I didn't want to break it or jeopardize what we'd built.

I don't know what made me realize I was ready to consider

having a second child—truly, I don't. Suddenly, it just felt right. Like our family was ready to expand.

And in the midst of the joy that came from expecting a new baby, tragedy struck and I lost my father.

My heart shattered. I had so much grief—and also so much work to do. Losing someone comes with a tremendous amount of paperwork and legal loopholes that no one tells you about. It's emotional. It's tedious. And I got to do it all while pregnant and caring for a toddler.

In the days leading up to my second daughter's birth, I have to confess that I was terrified. I was scared that having her would dramatically alter my relationship with my first child. I was still processing the grief of losing my own parent. The two were tangled and mixed up in my head—sadness and joy. Love and loss.

Will it change everything? Can I love them both enough?

Those thoughts ran circles in my mind. And to be honest? I think that's a fear most parents have—because babies *do* change everything.

But there's no way to put into words the feeling that happens when you hold both of your children for the first time and realize exactly how big love can get.

Love multiplies. It expands.

Some of the most joyous moments of my parenting journey have been watching my children love one another (when they're not fighting). The way they care they take of one another, the protectiveness, the love. It's enough to make your heart burst sometimes.

That's what I got to witness when my two girls met for the first time. I got to watch love grow and expand and, in turn, it healed me a little. It took away the questions—or at least, some of them.

The questions never fully go away, of course. But something else takes shape in their place: trust. Not trust that everything will go smoothly, but that somehow we'll stretch to meet it. That whatever happens, love will make space.

And it does.

9

Learning to Trust Myself

P eople used to tell me I was such a calm and gentle parent. That I never yelled (my kids will tell you otherwise, now), even in the most stressful of moments. They were amazed at my composure, at my calm. And I think, in part, that my forced, outward calm came because I was trying so hard to take it slow, to do everything exactly right. To not mess up.

I remember those first few days of my oldest daughter's life— how I would look at her lying next to me and feel a wave of shock. *Her parents aren't coming to pick her up,* I'd think, *because we're her parents.* It felt surreal.

Those early months were filled with pressure—pressure I placed on myself to get it right—and pressure from those around us, all of whom had opinions. We fed her on a schedule. We measured how much milk she got. I built a spreadsheet to track everything. Sometimes (and I hate to admit this), we even refused to feed her *because it wasn't time yet.*

But when my second baby came, I was different. Not because I suddenly had all the answers, but because I had made enough mistakes the first time to realize that there was no perfect formula (pun intended). There was only trial and error. There was only love and learning.

With my second, I got a sidecar sleeper and—more often than not—pulled her right into bed with me. Why? It was easier for both of us. More soothing. Less jarring. I gave up burping during late-night feedings. Why? She didn't get gassy. I know, I know—you're *supposed* to burp them every single time. You're *supposed* to let them self-soothe. But do you really have to?

She didn't get gassy. She didn't spit up her food. She was soothed and just settled back in to sleep. And so did I. And that was a beautiful thing that we both needed.

And guess what else? I didn't change her diaper at every feeding or the moment that little strip turned blue. (*Do you know how much those tiny diapers can hold? It's incredible.*) I stopped counting every poop and every pee. I stopped tracking. I deleted the spreadsheet.

In short, I gave myself the freedom to sit back and enjoy her. To meet her where she was. To listen to her needs instead of listening to all the noise.

And she demanded that we listen. She came into the world quick and hard and fast and in her own way. From the start, she refused to let the trail be blazed for her—she demanded that we learn *her*, not just lean on what we thought we already knew from her sister.

If it worked for Charlotte, it was almost guaranteed not to work for Vivi.

My first baby had wanted nothing more than to be snuggled after she was fed. My second? She wanted to be burped (sometimes) and laid down by herself—but not too far away. She needed space and closeness, both at once. It was like she wanted to bask in the glow of being just a little milk drunk, soaking it in alone, but still within reach.

Of course, now that she's older, we know she can be easily overstimulated. And I think some part of her always carried that self-awareness.

Parenting has a way of teaching you that you know absolutely nothing—and weirdly, there's beauty in that. My second baby taught me that and, in teaching me that valuable lesson, she freed me. I got to try new things. I got to fail. I got to pick myself up and try again.

And no—before those words can be twisted, we weren't "trying again" with a second baby. Please never confuse that. I have four beautiful children, and I have four beautiful children *on purpose.*

But after my first, I was more open to finding my own way. I still listened to advice, but I felt less beholden to it. That doesn't mean people's opinions didn't get under my skin—they did, and sometimes they still do.

And that doesn't mean I didn't listen to it sometimes. The difference is that now I know that I have the right to take the space and ask: why? Why do I have to wake her up to burp her if she's comfortable? Why do I have to change her diaper the moment it's wet if she's not uncomfortable? Why can't she sleep with me? Why?

Two and a half years into motherhood, I was starting—just *starting*—to feel like I had some idea what I was doing. And even when my second daughter proved me wrong again and again (because, of course, she did), I had something I didn't have the first time: trust.

Not in outcomes. Not in parenting books. In myself. At least a little. And it turns out, that's enough.

29

10

Toddlers, Chaos and the Myth of Control

I f I'm honest, I don't remember much about my first child's toddlerhood. I know that's probably not fair, but at the same time, we were in the thick of the newborn haze with our second baby. Quite frankly, I think she was just a really easy toddler. Either that, or she was so terrible I've blocked it all out. I choose to believe it was the first one.

But when I think about toddlerhood—like the quintessential, textbook kind of toddlerhood—a specific moment with my second daughter comes to mind.

It was a rainy day, and we were headed to the home improvement store. You know the kind—concrete floors, high ceilings, weird lighting that makes everything feel more dramatic than it actually is. My husband dropped me and the girls off at the front door so we wouldn't get wet.

(Spoiler: he was carrying the brand-new baby. But we'll talk about him later.)

Inside, my three-year-old spotted a shopping cart and immediately declared, "I want that cart."

The problem? The cart she wanted had someone else's stuff in it. And the "someone else" was standing just a few feet away browsing a shelf. "We can't have that cart," I said calmly. "It belongs to someone else."

She lost it.

I mean lost it in the way only a toddler can. Screaming. Flailing. Kicking. Pure chaos.

And then—because this story gets better—my husband walked in just in time to see her bolt away from us, straight into the center of a massive ring of grills. You know the setup they do in stores for the summer season? Dozens of grills arranged in a circle, each one touching at the corners, forming a big, enclosed space with price signs all around it. There was a tiny gap—just big enough for a small child to squeeze through. And squeeze through she did.

Right into the middle.

Where she sat down and screamed. I mean *really* screamed.

I couldn't reach her. I couldn't climb in after her. I couldn't talk her down. So, I did what every rational parent would do in that moment: I looked at my husband, handed him the baby and our other daughter, and said: "Take the others and save yourselves."

Because in that moment, I knew—really knew—that I was not in control.

We like to think we are. Or maybe we just hope we are. We think that with the right words, the right tone, the right disciplinary tactic, we can steer our children exactly where we want them to go. That we can avoid embarrassment or pain or disaster through sheer force of will. But the moment you bring another human into your life and agree to be responsible for them forever, you give up control.

And here's the kicker: they don't have it either.

That's the truth no one wants to say out loud. Toddlers don't *want* to be out of control any more than we do. But they are. Their emotions are bigger than their brains. Their limbs are faster than their logic. Their bodies carry the full force of chaos—and they have no idea what to do with it.

So sometimes they scream in the middle of a grill circle.

And sometimes, all you can do is sit quietly and wait.

Eventually, she crawled back out to me. I held her. We talked about not running away and not stealing other people's carts. She got a snuggle. I got a moment to reflect on the absurdity of it all.

And then—because this is how toddlers work—we repeated some version of that moment a hundred more times in the coming years. Probably a thousand. (She was a challenging kid.)

But something in me had shifted. I stopped expecting to control her. And instead, I started looking for my focal point. That one thing I could return to in the middle of the swirling storm. Not the perfect parenting tactic. Not the script from a book. Not even the illusion of calm. Just presence. Just love. Just one deep breath, and then another.

(And frequent venting sessions to friends and family.)

I couldn't control her—but I could anchor myself in the moment. And that, it turns out, is (usually) enough to get you through until the next storm.

And another storm *will* come. Again and again and again.

Brace yourself.

11

They'll Do It In Their Own Time

My first child walked at nine and a half months. I was unprepared. With the others, I knew better than to expect a full year of baby bliss.

By ten months with our second, my husband was worried. "Is she okay?" he asked.

"She'll do it in her own time," I told him, reminding him that most kids don't walk until around 12 months—or later. She walked a couple of weeks later. Our next two walked right around 11 months each.

Our first was also the only one who was easy to potty train. She just took to it—after first tragically soiling a pair of Elsa underwear, a trauma from which she barely recovered.

The Elsa underwear was a special treat—ones that my very non-feminine teen now grimaces to recall. But back then, they were incredible. She picked them out herself (and let me tell you, they were 1,000 times more expensive than any of the other options at the time).

"Now," we reminded her regularly, "you have to listen to your body and go to the bathroom when you wear your Elsa

33

underwear."

Not more than a day into this new routine, she came running into our room in tears. "I pooped *on Elsa!*" she sobbed. It was one of those parenting moments where you simply *cannot* look at one another—because if you do, it's over. We would have broken down laughing until we cried. In fact, our eyes *were* full of tears, just trying to hold it in.

"Oh no!" we exclaimed, doing our best serious parent faces. "You didn't listen to your body!"

Of course, we consoled her and cleaned (ugh) the soiled underwear. But it was about the only time that happened. She had learned her lesson—and from that day forward, she was generally accident-free.

The others? I used to joke that I was pretty sure they wouldn't go to college in diapers. *Pretty* sure. Definitely not convinced.

Our second child would calmly bring us her soiled underwear and ask for a new pair.

Our third hid his in the closet (yes, gross).

And our fourth? She refused altogether—tore off her underwear and peed on the living room rug.

With her, I finally snapped. "You're going to daycare in underwear tomorrow," I told her.

"Why?" she asked, genuinely curious.

"Because," I said, hating every word of it, "you're a big kid. And it's time."

She was three and a half. And I was absolutely feeling the pressure of her still wearing diapers—not from her, but from everyone around us.

That same pressure had followed us with our son—and I broke under it with him too and pushed him, hard, to potty train. The truth is that the way we pushed him to potty train is probably why he started hiding his accidents. We made him feel ashamed that he wasn't doing things "on schedule," and I regret that to this day.

Ironically, our daughter took to it right away. Apparently, going to daycare in underwear was the trick. But the lesson remains: she did it when she was ready. Just like they all did.

There are milestones that all kids are "supposed" to hit. And yes—some of them matter. But most of them? They're just averages. Guidelines. Not gospel.

Sleep regressions? Mine never hit them when other people's kids did.

Teeth? Not until nearly a year old.

There's so much pressure on parents to compare and measure and monitor as if childhood were some kind of competition.

It's not. Stop it.

Let them be them. Let them grow and stretch and stumble and bloom.

And unless something is truly, medically concerning? Let them do it in their own time. They'll be happier. And—trust me—so will you.

12

You Don't Know Everything

We were driving downtown—my husband, our daughters, and I—when my oldest announced loudly and proudly from the back seat: "Pterodactyls are *not* dinosaurs."

"Of course they are," I told her. "Pterodactyls are definitely dinosaurs."

"No," she said. "They're not. They're cousins to dinosaurs."

We went back and forth like this for a while. I was calm at first, but my voice started getting tight, like it does when I think I'm being patient, but I'm actually losing my mind.

I *knew* I was right. I mean, I'm the adult. I've read books. I've seen museum exhibits. I've watched *Jurassic Park*. Pterodactyls are dinosaurs... right?

Finally, I took a deep breath and reminded myself that I was the actual grown-up in this situation. So I said, "You know what? I think we're just going to have to agree to disagree."

"Yes," she agreed immediately. "Because you're wrong."

There was such certainty in her tone and I could see her glancing out the window, so pleased with herself. In the seat next to me, I could feel my husband tense up, like he was waiting to see if I was about to completely unravel. And to be honest, I was close. But I took another breath. Because, again, I'm the adult, right? I needed to act like it. Not fight with an elementary school child. (Preschool, maybe? The details are fuzzy.)

Days later, I looked it up. And you know what?

Pterodactyls are *not* dinosaurs. They are, in fact, close cousins to dinosaurs.

I had been so confident. So certain. But I was wrong.

That was the moment I realized that sometimes these tiny humans we're raising know more than we do. They are soaking in information constantly—from school, daycare, books, conversations, television, and who knows what else. They're surrounded by facts we didn't even know they were absorbing.

They are smart. Often, they are more curious and more open than we are. And sometimes? They're right. Even when it bruises our adult pride.

What I've learned—what I'm still learning—is that part of parenting is knowing when to pause. When to stop and really listen. When to say, "Huh. I didn't know that." Or even better: "Let's look it up together."

Because our kids have so much to teach us, even as we're trying to guide them toward adulthood.

And if you ever find yourself in a car with a five-year-old confidently telling you you're wrong—well, buckle up.

You might be.

III

Roots and Wings

"Everyone should have kids. They are the greatest joy in the world. But they are also terrorists. You'll realize this as soon as they are born and they start using sleep deprivation to break you." – Ray Romano

13

To Jude Alan Edward

You came into the world fast and fierce, but only after keeping us waiting—and wondering—for what felt like forever.

You were born yesterday at 8:49 PM, weighing 8 lbs. 8 oz. and measuring 21.5 inches long. Your name carries deep roots on both sides of our family: Alan for your dad and grandfathers, Edward for my dad, and Jude Alan because it sounds an awful lot like June Allyn—a quiet nod to your great-grandmother.

Your birth was preceded by a long, emotional day and an even longer emotional week. Just days before your due date, both Charlotte and Vivi came down with the flu. It was a bad year for the flu and kids were getting sick and hospitalized in record numbers. I was nine months pregnant, exhausted, terrified, and doing everything I could to keep everyone comfortable and safe—including you, still tucked inside. With their diagnosis, you moved out of an optimal birthing position and my body refused to let you come out of the relative safety I provided you. Not until your girls were healthy and well.

And then, once they healed, every night for days, contractions would start and last for hours—then disappear. I felt defeated, confused, and at times totally overwhelmed. By the morning of your due date, I had hit my wall. I called Emily, our midwife, and told her I needed help. I needed you *out*. And then I wrestled with that feeling all day. After waiting more than 41 weeks for both of your sisters, choosing to intervene at 40 weeks felt like a kind of failure. But something in me knew—it was time.

Emily arrived around 11:30 AM and found that I was already 2–3 centimeters dilated. You had moved up high in my belly, which was actually a good sign—it meant you were no longer in a posterior position (like she had feared) and were finally in the right spot for labor to begin. With careful thought and consent, we started a few gentle methods to help things along: herbs, homeopathics, walking, resting, waiting.

Contractions came back, but again, they didn't go anywhere. So around 3:00 PM, we sent your dad out to buy castor oil (not a thing to do without medical supervision). He came home and, a little grossed out, made me a castor egg (yes, that's a thing). I ate it with a prayer and a little bit of desperation as Emily looked me in the eye and made me promise not to hate her when labor started, because it was going to come on strong—and fast.

She was right.

After some calm hours and Anthony Bourdain on TV, and listening to the song "Closing Time" on a loop, my contractions suddenly picked up speed. Sometime before 7:00 PM, Emily declared I was officially in labor and called in reinforcements. Anna, a local nurse-midwife and a bright light during Charlotte's birth, arrived just in time. And then—just like that—my contractions paused again. My body has always had a flair for drama.

Emily slipped me another round of herbs and left the room

with Anna to give me some space. That's when it happened—just after 7:00, the first *real* contraction hit. It was strong and painful, and to be honest, I welcomed it. Three minutes later came another. Then they started coming every 1–2 minutes with almost no break between. Emily looked at me and said, "If you need to call anyone, now's the time."

We called my mom. We called Christy, our doula. And we quickly realized there wasn't time to fill the birthing tub. The bathtub would have to do.

The next half hour was a blur of hot water, dim lights, and deep breathing. I moved from tub to bed and back again. Christy pressed on a spot near my ankle that helped me stay grounded, and Emily reminded me to breathe through each contraction—breathe you down, not tense up, not push too early. It hurt, but in a way that felt purposeful. I wasn't afraid. I was ready.

I was surrounded—your dad, my mom, Emily, Anna, Christy—each one of them encouraging me, holding me, and helping me stay focused. I've never felt more supported in my entire life. At some point, my body started pushing. I remember hearing Emily say your chin was out, and I knew I had to slow down. I had to breathe and deliver you with intention. And I did. I felt each part of you enter the world—and then, finally, the rush of relief as you slid into my arms.

You were perfect.

Later, we learned that you were measuring about 41 weeks according to the Ballard scale, and that my placenta was starting to calcify. It was done. And so were we. That knowledge quieted the voice in my head that had been telling me I gave up too soon. I hadn't. I had listened to my body—and to you.

Jude, your birth taught me that there's strength in surrender.

That just because something is fast doesn't mean it's rushed. That just because I asked for help doesn't mean I failed.

You arrived in your own way and your own time—and it was exactly what we needed.

We needed *you*.

Love always,
  Mama

14

Firsts (Again)

My children are all roughly three years apart—and quite frankly, that's a little bit by design. The truth is, even with two full-time incomes, there was no way we could afford to have two kids in daycare at once. So, when we decided to add a third child to our family, our first was just about ready for kindergarten.

No one really tells you how complicated it is to pick a school for your child these days. Or maybe they do, and I just didn't listen. Either way, I was overwhelmed. We live in an area that allows families to request schools outside their assigned district—something called "school of choice"—and suddenly it felt like the options were endless, and the stakes impossibly high.

We visited at least three or four elementary schools before landing on a dual language immersion program. Why? Because children pick up new languages more easily than adults, and even if she didn't retain every word of Spanish into adulthood, research shows that learning a second language as a child supports cognitive development and brain growth. (Look it up—or don't. Either way, it felt like the right call.)

We picked the school. I bought her outfits. We packed her backpack and met her teacher. We set alarms and laid out shoes the night before. And then, on that first morning, we walked together to the bus stop.

What no one warned me about—what no school checklist or parenting article could prepare me for—was what it would feel like to watch my daughter climb onto a big yellow bus and drive away with someone I had never met.

I thought I was ready. But when the bus pulled off, I broke. The sob came from somewhere deep in my chest, and to this day, I can hardly think about that moment without crying. That tiny human, whose hand I had held across every street and whose hair I had brushed that morning with extra care, was suddenly moving out into the world without me. It was just kindergarten—but it felt like the first real letting go.

Yes, I know it's foreshadowing for all the goodbyes to come. College. Adulthood. Independence. But I wasn't there yet. I was here. In this moment. On the sidewalk. Watching my heart drive away.

I did what any logical mother would do. I sent my husband after her. I asked him to follow the bus in the car and attend the orientation for nervous parents of kindergartners, while I stayed home with the toddler and the new baby—watching the clock and waiting on the front porch for her to come home.

It was a long (half) day.

I would love to tell you that kindergarten was everything we hoped for. That she thrived. That she loved it from day one. But the truth is, it was hard.

She is—and I hope always will be—an incredibly sensitive child. Her heart aches for others. She takes things personally

46

that some kids can easily brush off. And in those early school days, she struggled. She was picked on. Bullied, even. And we spent many evenings sitting together on the couch, gently helping her navigate the heartbreak of living in a world that isn't always kind.

And yet—through it all—she kept turning toward us.

That's the part I come back to. The part that steadied me. Even as she was learning to spread her wings, she came home when things got hard. And I think that's the lesson: we have to let them go. We have to let them fly. But we also have to help them build roots strong enough, deep enough, that they know exactly where to land when life gets rough.

And we do that by loving them. Deeply. Unconditionally. With open arms.

Firsts don't get easier just because it's your second or third child. Each one feels new, because it is. Each child is their own unfolding. And as parents, we are asked—again and again—to love, to release, and to remain a safe place to return to.

Even when they're just five.

Even when it's only the bus stop.

Even when we're crying on the sidewalk.

Especially then

15

Let Them Climb

There's a photo I keep coming back to. My daughter is halfway up a tornado-shaped climbing structure at her elementary school. It was yellow metal—the structure. She's looking up at me, smiling in pure joy. The playground was quiet and empty around us as I snapped the picture, but I knew the playground wasn't always this way. And certainly not this structure.

No, not this structure. This one had to be a kid favorite. Always (I assumed) swarmed during recess. I imagine the clatter of sneakers against bars, the shriek of laughter echoing across the blacktop. It looked a little like a tornado, but to them, it was a tower, a mountain, a spaceship, a castle.

And to me, in those early years, it was a test.

No matter their age, each of my children was intrinsically drawn to this piece of playground equipment, almost as though it was magnetic. Could I stand back and watch? Could I let them climb without calling out, *Be careful!* every thirty seconds?

In the beginning, no. I couldn't. Definitely not.

In fact, I hovered. I hovered like it was my job—because in so

48

many ways, it was. I was the protector, the safety net, the extra set of eyes. My entire body would tense as my child reached for the next rung, one shoe slipping a little before finding grip. My hand would instinctively shoot out, ready to steady. Ready to catch.

I think, in those days, I might have climbed more playground equipment than my children. And let me tell you what, it's not easy—even as a relatively petite person—to make your way on equipment that's not built for you.

And then one day—I didn't. Not because I didn't care, but because I finally understood something: the equipment wasn't for me. It was for them. Moreover, the goal was never to keep them on the ground. The goal was to let them climb.

That didn't mean I stopped watching. It didn't mean I stopped worrying. I still gasped when they reached the top and turned around with outstretched arms and wobbling legs. But I also started cheering. Not just for making it, but for trying. For having confidence in themselves. For being courageous enough to explore. To reach. For assessing the risk and saying, *I can do this.*

That confidence—mine in them, theirs in themselves—wasn't built all at once.

It grew, rung by rung. Every scraped knee. Every almost-fall. Every triumphant smile. And with it grew something else: a quiet understanding that I didn't have to be at the top anymore. I could stand back. I could let them figure it out.

Because the truth is, we all have our yellow tornado and whether we like it or not, they climb higher when they know you believe they can.

And while I'm stepping back now, watching from below instead of standing at the top, I know this isn't the end of the climb—not for them, and not for me. Every new challenge, every risk taken, every step upward is part of the journey we share.

True, my role changes, but my love and belief remain the same: steady, patient, and ready to catch them if they fall. Because sometimes, letting them climb means trusting that they're strong enough to find their own way—and that's the greatest gift I can give.

16

Stop. Regulate and Reframe.

I remember one night when Jude was still a toddler—struggling to fall asleep, tossing and turning in his bed. Suddenly, he started crying out, "I don't know HOW to sleep! I don't know HOW to GO TO SLEEP!"

In that moment, I felt that familiar tug—because we've all been there. The helplessness when something so simple and necessary feels impossible. The pressure to "just do it" that somehow makes everything worse.

Instead, I gathered him up, held him close, and said softly, "That's okay, baba. We won't go to sleep then. Let's not do that right now. Let's just snuggle. You know how to snuggle—in fact, you're the very best at snuggling."

His body relaxed, his tears slowed, and before long, he was sound asleep, nestled in my arms.

That moment taught me something that should have been obvious: sometimes our job isn't to fix the feeling—it's to hold it.

He didn't need me to teach him how to sleep—he needed me to remind him that he was safe. That he wasn't alone. That he already had what he needed.

When the path forward seems blocked, when anxiety or frustration take over, sometimes the best way through is to shift the frame. To say, "It's okay to pause. It's okay to be exactly where you are." To remind them that they already have what they need—love, presence, safety—even if the goal feels far away.

We talk a lot about self-regulation in kids. But before they can do that, they have to learn how to borrow calm from someone else. That night, he borrowed mine.

This isn't just a parenting trick. It's a lesson in compassion and patience that I'm learning alongside my children. The truth is that life rarely moves in a straight line. We all have moments when we don't know how to sleep, or how to calm down, or how to be who we want to be.

And that's the real work, sometimes—not letting go or stepping back, but staying close enough to carry them through the storm. It's about creating space to breathe, to reset, to soften into what is instead of fighting against it. It's about reframing and regulating.

And in those moments, the love that underpins it all becomes visible—a quiet strength that doesn't demand perfection or quick fixes but simply holds us steady while we find our way.

So here's to the quiet work of parenting. The reframes. The resets. The nights when snuggling is the solution. The moments when love whispers, "You're safe," before sleep finally comes.

17

Who They're Becoming

There's something almost sacred about the stretch of years when a child begins to show you who they really are—not just who they are to you.

I remember when my oldest decided, in fourth grade, that she was going to play the violin in the school orchestra. She brought the battered, school instrument home from school, cradled it like it was something precious, and excitedly showed us what she had learned so far.

We didn't have any musical background—nothing to compare it to, no real frame of reference—but we listened. And, as the weeks wore on, we listened more closely. There was something in the way she played, even early on, that made us wonder if maybe this wasn't just a school program—it was something more.

She wanted to keep the instrument over the summer. Her teacher said yes, if we found her lessons. So, we did. I sent a clip of her playing to a friend who used to be a violinist, just to ask. "She's actually pretty good," my friend told me. "Better than you'd expect for her age and how little time she's had."

I didn't quite know what to do with that. I had assumed she'd be like me—earnest, clumsy, well-intentioned. But she wasn't me. She was herself. And, it seemed, she was a budding musician.

The same thing happened again in fifth grade, when she fell in love with soccer. She begged to join a team and then begged again to move up to travel soccer. We knew nothing about the game. My only advice was that she couldn't use her hands—and then (obviously) her little sister announced she wanted to be a goalie, and then I was completely out of wisdom.

They kept surprising me. They still do.

And somewhere in the middle of all that stretching and unfolding, we started following them—not the other way around. We went to concerts, sat on cold bleachers, Googled soccer rules, and found ourselves pulled into a world we didn't even know to want.

Recently, we ventured to our local symphony and sat, in awe, listening to Yo-Yo Ma perform alongside them. The music was extraordinary. But what struck me more than anything was this: we were there because of our children. They were the ones who brought us. They were the ones who opened this door.

And it made me wonder: how many of the best parts of our lives begin that way? Not because we plan them, but because we follow someone we love through a door they're excited to open.

I used to think it was my job to shape them. But now I think it's more about bearing witness. About paying attention. About recognizing that they are not extensions of us, but whole people—becoming. And we get to watch.

Aren't we the lucky ones?

18

The Tutu

Shortly after my son started preschool—fresh out of the pandemic, with a brand-new baby sister at home—he fell head over heels for a green and black tutu that used to belong to his sister Viviana.

He wore it constantly. It became part of every outfit, every day. It wasn't a security blanket, exactly. It was more like a statement. A signal. This is who I am. This is what I like.

When I asked him why, he said it makes him feel beautiful. He told me that when "his girls" dress up, they look absolutely beautiful, and he wants to look that way too.

And it's not just dresses. He wears boys' dress clothes too. But for really special occasions? When he wants to feel just amazing? It's a dress. It's doing his nails and brushing his hair.

His little personality didn't conform to the world's expectations. And, honestly, the world didn't quite know what to do with that.

My older daughter is like that too. She refuses to wear anything remotely "girly." She recently chopped her hair short and fully embraces a more masculine style. I've watched her navigate that space, and it's not always easy. But I'm realizing it's often even harder for my son.

In those early weeks of preschool, when he showed up every day in his tutu, some of the kids were kind—really excited about his style, curious, even a little inspired. But some weren't. And the teachers? Well, when I spoke with them, one told me, "Well, if he's going to dress that way, he'll need to expect those types of comments."

That moment hit me hard. It was the first time I had to push back—I mean really push back—against social norms on behalf of my kids. It wasn't the last.

What really made it clear to me, though, was realizing how much kids are parrots. They're repeating what they hear from the adults around them. And sure, as a parent, I can gently redirect those little voices when they stumble. But it's the adults—teachers, caregivers, community members—who need the bigger mindset shift.

And that's harder.

Here's the thing: I used to teach gender studies. I have an actual degree in it. I've read the theory, led the discussions, and done the work.

Teaching gender and women's studies, I was used to a certain kind of pushback—often intellectual, sometimes resistant, but mostly within a willing audience. Frankly, many of my students came because they wanted to learn. That's not always the case outside the classroom.

The push back here? It's different. It's more raw. Less thoughtful. Sometimes it's dismissive. Sometimes it's just silent discomfort.

But this—this is the real work.

Because it's about more than theory. It's about my child's

daily life, his safety, his sense of belonging. All of theirs, really. Because when they see that we stand up for him, they know we've got their backs too. We're in their corner. No matter what.

And that makes it impossible to turn away.

Having a beautiful, imaginative, real-life child who defies social norms? That stretches you. Even when you didn't think it would.

And so, there's also been a reckoning in our house—a rethinking. A mix of emotions swirling inside me.

There's pride. Pride that my children are confident enough to show up in the world exactly as they are.

There's disappointment—at myself, for sometimes having to pause and remind my own brain that they are perfect, exactly as they are.

There's frustration. With a world that still struggles to accept difference. That tries to box them in before they've even had the chance to bloom.

And maybe, most of all, there's love.

Love that's learning to stretch. Love that's learning to listen. Love that doesn't care what they wear—but deeply cares how the world treats them when they do. Love that is willing to show up—in big ways and small—to let them know that they matter and they're perfect exactly as they are.

IV

The Juggling Act

"It just occurred to me that the majority of my diet is made up of the foods that my kid didn't finish." –
Carrie Underwood

19

To Margaret Richelle

You were born just after midnight on July 5, 2021, in the thick of a global pandemic and a relentless heat wave. You made your entrance at 1:20 a.m., weighing 8 pounds, 5 ounces, with a head of red hair and a name that had been waiting for you for years—and fireworks exploded in the night sky as you took your first breath. How many kids can say that?

We didn't know if you'd be a boy or a girl, so your name—Margaret Richelle—was something we held close but loosely. It was passed down through a line of strong women and stitched together with deep family ties: Margaret from great-great-grandmothers and aunts; Richelle for your Aunt Sissy, whose birthday you now share, and as a nod to your great-grandfather. It was the only name we agreed on this time. Fitting, really. You arrived with certainty in some very uncertain times.

Your head had been nestled low for weeks before your birth, which meant I had been waddling and wildly uncomfortable as the summer sweltered on. We'd tentatively scheduled an induction for July 9—past your due date—but when I spoke with one of the midwives on July 4, we bumped it to the morning of July 5. I half-joked that I'd try to go into labor on my own over the weekend. I didn't expect it to work.

But you had other plans.

That evening, while we debated where to watch the fireworks, contractions quietly began stringing themselves together—eight minutes apart, then six, then three. I thought they might fizzle out like they had so many nights before. Still, we packed the kids in the car and watched the sky light up from church parking lots and quiet streets while I breathed through what I now know was early labor.

Eventually I asked to go home. The contractions were steady now, growing sharper. I called the hospital, and they told us to come in. We tucked your siblings into our bed, sang them a few songs, and slipped out—leaving them in the care of our dear friend Jacci—with one quick return for my forgotten purse, of course.

When we arrived at the hospital, I was five centimeters dilated. We weren't sure if this was really it, but they admitted me since I was already scheduled to be induced in a few hours anyway. The unit was busy that night, yet somehow we ended up with an extraordinary nurse named Felissa who cared for me with such calm and confidence that I still feel grateful thinking of her.

Stubborn as you are, you made me shift my birth plan immediately. When we got to the hospital, you were experiencing tachycardia, which meant I needed an IV and constant monitoring throughout labor. Surprisingly, the sound of your heartbeat echoing through the room turned out to be more calming than the best labor music.

Labor picked up quickly. I spent time on the yoga ball, then the tub, and eventually found myself in that familiar storm of doubt and intensity. I told your dad I couldn't do it anymore. That I needed something—an epidural, a break, relief. Felissa sat beside me and talked me through every option with such gentleness that I felt steadier just hearing her voice. She checked me: eight centimeters with a bulging bag of water.

"We can still do the epidural," she said, "or we can break your water and deliver a baby."

I looked at her and said, "Let's deliver the baby." It was the right call.

Jenna, the midwife, arrived, broke my waters, and suggested laboring upright to help move you down, but I remembered how gravity hadn't worked in my favor with your brother. We adjusted the plan, and with the help of a beanbag and some clever bed angles, I turned onto my side.

Within seconds, everything shifted and you began crowning. None of the team was ready and I struggled to find words to tell (lest you be born into a beanbag). My mind was blank—just pure sensation and urgency. "The baby is coming!" I finally managed, and everyone sprang into motion. Jenna rushed to pull on gloves. Felissa moved the beanbag from between my legs. It took just a few strong pushes and, with my hand on my stomach, I felt you slide into the world. And then, just like that, you were in my arms.

Fireworks exploded outside the window as I looked down at your face. Then I checked under the towel to see who you were. What name I should call you. "Hi, Maggie," I whispered. And just like that, you were here.

You are my only child for whom I cut the cord. There's so much packed into that, but I'll save that for another day.

Every child changes the family. But you, sweet girl, arrived in the thick of a season already bursting at the seams. You didn't pause the chaos; you joined it. And yet somehow, you softened it too. You've always been able to keep pace with the rhythm around you while carving out your own space inside it. It's a special kind of grace (some might say stubbornness), and you've had it from the start.

And guess what? We love you.

Love,
  Mama

20

The Last Firsts

When my son was a baby, I thought he would be our last.

One to four kids—that was the plan, ideally with both genders represented. His birth checked every box. We felt complete. And so, I savored the moments of his early life with the quiet ache of someone aware they were saying goodbye in real time.

I held him longer. Rocked him more slowly. Paid attention. But I also tried not to mark the endings. Was this the last time he nursed? The last time he needed me to sing that song? The last time he would rub my knuckle across his lip?

I wanted to let the moments pass through me gently, without the grief I knew would come if I named them too sharply.

And then, when he was three and a half, I found myself standing in the doorway of our bedroom, a T-shirt that read *Big Brother* in my hand. I tossed it across the room to my husband.

"For real?" he asked, a slow grin spreading across his face.

"For real," I said.

And just like that, we entered the (second) season of Last

Firsts.

But first—our baby had to grow up.

It's funny how the baby of the family never really seems to grow up. Not because they aren't growing, but because there's no one after them to show you just how much they've changed. They stay small longer in your eyes.

That illusion broke the moment our fourth was born.

Our toddler, who had seemed so little just the day before, suddenly looked enormous. Capable. Grown. His limbs seemed longer, his cheeks less round. The contrast undid me.

He was my last.

Until he wasn't.

And that simple shift cracked something open in me.

Because I wasn't the same this time.

This birth—this new baby—came in the middle of a global pandemic, during a relentless summer heat wave, in a world that no longer felt solid under our feet. The backdrop wasn't just different—it was disorienting. The rhythms of support I had relied on in the past weren't available. No one passed the baby around. There were no visitors in the hospital. No crowds of family. Just masks. Isolation. A strange, sacred quiet.

There was something beautiful in that quiet, and I grew to understand the *staying-in* period that many cultures cherish— this time to revere, to adjust, to get to know one another without the rush of expectations. It gave us precious time to savor these fleeting moments, to settle into a new kind of intimacy that might have otherwise been lost.

And something in me changed, too.

Maybe it was age. Or maybe it was experience. Maybe it was the fragility of the world around us. But I found myself holding this baby—and this season—with new hands. Not clinging,

66

exactly. But not rushing either.

I took a full twelve weeks of maternity leave (not fully paid, obviously) and turned work off. I let the laundry pile up so I could lay down and nap. I moved through the world slowly.

I knew this time how quickly it would all pass. How fleeting the newborn sounds are. How fast the soft skin firms. How final some firsts can feel once they're gone.

And so I began to mark them:

The last time I swaddled her in my favorite swaddle.

The last time I snapped that tiny pajama size.

The last time I packed away clothes I knew I'd never use again. Ever.

But with each Last First came something new. A shift. A discovery. A milestone I might've missed in the rush of early motherhood the first time around. With this final baby, I wasn't just raising her. I was witnessing us—our whole family—grow and stretch and take shape around her presence.

It's tempting to see the end of babyhood as a kind of loss. And in some ways, it is.

But there's also something profoundly beautiful about seeing a season close, and knowing you gave it everything. That you stayed awake to it. That you paid attention. That you learned how to let go slowly.

These are our Last Firsts. And the piece I realize now is that they aren't an ending—they're a beginning, because Firsts never really end, and there's always a new one just around the bend

21

Big Kids, Big Feelings

Becoming a family of six wasn't automatic. My husband and I stood on rather different sides of that decision for a while.

One thing he kept coming back to was the idea of starting over. "Things are just starting to get easier," he'd say. The gist was this: our kids were becoming more self-sufficient, more resilient, more their own people—and that gave *us* more freedom, too.

We were moving beyond the stage of midnight feedings, toddler tantrums, and diaper changes. Circling back felt, to him, like going in reverse.

But I kept reminding him: *big kids come with big feelings.*

We were about to enter a stage of parenting that was just as intense—but less visible. One where a hug and a kiss wouldn't fix it. One where you can't just distract them from the hard stuff, because the hard stuff is bigger now. Deeper. More complicated.

In 2023, as our toddler approached #threenager status, our son started kindergarten, and our oldest daughter started middle school. Yes, we timed that one poorly. Yes, I'm grateful that our second was on relatively stable ground during this shaky period in our lives.

Putting your child on the school bus for the first time doesn't get easier over time—it still takes a chunk out of you. But sending one into *middle school*? That's another kind of heartbreak altogether. And that fall, I did both. On the same day.

Here's the thing: if there's one place I'd never choose to return to, it's middle school. Can we all just agree that this stage of life is wildly unfair? New building, new schedule, new friends— and just when you think they're adjusting, we throw hormones into the mix.

It's cruel.

Truthfully, I don't know if I'll ever stop hating middle school. Not because of the academics, but because of what it does to kids' sense of self. How quickly they learn to shrink or perform. How fast they go from carefree to careful.

My daughter entered middle school with some excitement— she'd made friends at orchestra camp over the summer—but there was trepidation, too. And while things seemed to start off okay, it didn't take long before the tension started to build. Friendships shifted. Drama bubbled up. The emotional stakes felt *so* high, *so* fast.

And as much as I hate to say it—I was right. The challenges she faced were deeper and more layered than anything her younger brother was working through in kindergarten. They still are. And someday, we'll walk all of them through those challenges.

There were moments that year when my daughter came home radiant, full of stories. But there were also days when her eyes clouded, and her jaw locked and I couldn't get more than a shrug.

She doesn't always tell me everything. But she tells me *enough*. Enough to know when something's off. Enough to know when to ask again, and when to stop asking and just sit beside her.

I wish I had answers. I wish I had a brilliant insight to wrap it all up with a bow. But the truth? The only way through this season is to *be there*.

Sometimes, my daughter hates me. I see it in her eyes. I feel it in the silence, in the tension in her shoulders. But I am there—annoyingly, persistently there. And over the past year, I think she's started to appreciate that.

I'm lucky: my kids still acknowledge me in public. They hug me (actually, quite a lot). They show affection to both me and their dad. I think one reason for that is we try to be honest because, at the end of the day, we're just big kids too. We have big feelings. And we don't always handle them well.

Just the other day, I yelled at my kids—specifically my daughters—about leaving the freezer open after getting ice cream. They swore they'd closed it but took the blame anyway. Ten minutes later, I realized: *I was the one who left it open.* I'd pulled out pizzas for dinner and handed one to the toddler to help carry it upstairs. I never closed the door.

So, I walked upstairs, called my girls over, and apologized. I told them I was wrong, and that when you're wrong, you have to *own it*.

My husband and I try to lead that way—with transparency. If we lose our tempers, we apologize. If we don't model what we ask of them—breathe, pause, take a walk—we admit it.

That's what's getting us through.

The truth is, I don't know how to parent a middle schooler. But I do know how to apologize when I mess up. I know how to sit with someone in silence. I know how to say, "You don't have to tell me everything, but I'm here if you want to."

I know how to make room for feelings that aren't convenient.

And maybe—just maybe—that's enough.

But it's definitely *not* easier. Not even a little.

22

In The Thick of It

W e were never going to co-sleep. That wasn't in the plans.

And yet, as our youngest approaches her fourth birthday, she's still snuggled tightly in my arms each night. My husband starts most evenings curled up beside our seven-year-old in his room.

How did we get here?

Ease. Convenience. Love. Exhaustion. Take your pick— it doesn't really matter. It's where we are. And, truthfully, I wouldn't trade it for the world even though I know the impact it's had on our marriage.

The truth is, it's just one of the many ways parenting has reshaped our marriage and our relationship—often in ways we never saw coming.

Remember *them*? The people who say, "Having kids is hard"?

What they meant was: **HARD**. All caps. Bold. Underlined.

And you just can't quite understand what that means until you're in it. Right in the thick of it.

Your relationship with your partner will suffer. I'm sorry—

but it will. Doubt me? Try having an uninterrupted conversation with a toddler around. I dare you. Let me know how that goes.

But here's the other truth: your relationship will also bloom—if you let it.

If you acknowledge what's not working but also look for the small ways you've learned to work together in the chaos... it will shift into something new.

Now, is it always going to be pretty? Absolutely not.

This seems like the perfect moment to pass on one of the best pieces of marriage advice I ever received. It went something like this:

"Everyone says you won't always *like* your spouse, but you'll always love them. That's crap. There will be days when you look at them and not only do you not like them—you won't even remember if, or why, you ever loved them."

And in those moments, you get to choose: move forward, or retreat.

My husband and I have hit those moments more than once over our nearly two decades together. And strangely enough, what keeps pulling us back together is our kids.

Neither of us can picture a world without their loud, loving, obnoxious, wonderful little selves—driving us completely insane, 24/7.

So we move forward. One foot at a time. One deep breath at a time.

And we've found that some people won't walk through the chaos with you.

But the ones who do? They're gold.

Those are the friends who will sit in the mess with you, who don't flinch when your kid is screaming mid-FaceTime, or when you can't even find an evening to get together that's less than a month out.

Those are the people we'll grow old and gray with.

As we begin easing our kids into their own rooms—slowly, because everything with kids is slow—I can feel the beginning of a new chapter.

A new era.

I don't know exactly what it will bring.

But I know we'll keep showing up in one way or another. And, really, I can't ask for more than that.

23

How We Do It

The first year my daughter Viviana danced in her ballet company's production of *The Nutcracker Kalamazoo,* we missed almost every rehearsal leading up to the actual show. That they still agreed to let her perform (after so many breathless apologies on my part) is still miraculous to me.

Ultimately, I'm pretty sure she didn't end up going onstage— she got sick that weekend—but that's another story.

The point is: we are not always on top of things. In this season of our lives, we have four kids. And between them, we juggle soccer, dance, orchestra, little league, and whatever else they dream up between now and next Tuesday. Sometimes it's multiple things at the same time, in different locations, on opposite sides of town. There are days we wave as we pass in the driveway as one of us returns from drop-off while the other heads to pick-up.

One day, my husband pulled in and I looked at him in bewilderment. "Why are you here?" I asked him.

"What…" he started to say, and then realized he was on pick-up duty for one of our children, who he obviously had not picked up. He drove away without another word as we all (well, most of us) laughed in the front yard.

To say we are busy would not be an overstatement.

And the wildest part is, our kids constantly ask to do more. "Can I try gymnastics?" Vivi asks me regularly, eyes wide with hope. I don't laugh, though I want to. I just give her the same answer I always do: "Sure—if you're ready to quit dance or soccer." That usually ends the conversation. "Never mind," she says, every time.

Life is full of boundaries, and some are harder to hold than others. But this one? This one is pretty easy. We don't have the time or the resources to say yes to everything and so they each get two things. And while that feels unfair sometimes—because I *want* them to try everything, to discover what lights them up—it just doesn't work.

The truth is we can't be everywhere, do everything, or pay for every single lesson, costume, and tournament fee. I want them to be well-rounded, but more than that, I want them to be well-rested. I want them to laugh in the car, not cry from exhaustion. I want family dinner once in a while. And that means saying no, even when yes would be more fun.

People ask me all the time, "How do you do it?" Four kids. Two jobs. Volunteer work. How does it all happen? I've started giving the same answer every time: one day at a time.

It's simple. It's not perfect. But it's what I can handle.

I love being a mom. I want my kids to have experiences, to be exposed to new things, to fall in love with art and music and movement. So, I say yes to sports and dance and orchestra sign-ups.

I also love my work—so I say yes to client projects and creative outlets that feed something in me beyond motherhood. I value friendship and marriage and my own mental health—so I try to make space for workouts, drinks with friends, and date nights.

But let me be very clear: this is not a perfectly curated calendar. This is not a color-coded success story (though the shared, family Google calendar is, in fact, color coded).

Do we oversleep sometimes? Yes. Definitely yes. (Every day, if you're me.) Recital weekends are chaos. Games always overlap. Uniforms get lost. Cleats get forgotten. Dinner is often whatever we can microwave in under three minutes or something that I can prep in the crock pot before work. Or Jimmy John's. We should really just buy a storefront at this point. But I digress...

Some days, I shut a door—any door—just to stand alone in silence and breathe. Other days, I lose it completely and yell. Like actually yell. Into the air. Into a pillow. Into the void. And then I apologize. I reset. I try again.

Still, in the middle of all the scheduling and the driving and the damage control, I catch these tiny, fleeting moments that tether me to the joy of it all. Like Maggie beaming on her way to school on a random Tuesday—just minutes after thrashing around like an angry octopus because her socks "felt weird."

Kids are emotional shapeshifters. But honestly, so are adults.

I say yes—probably more than I should. I pack the snacks and forget the permission slips (why are there so many permission slips?). I cheer from the sidelines. I take the pictures. I wipe the tears. I show up (sometimes late) but I show up.

And I keep going.

One day at a time.

24

Maybe They're My Growth Mindset

Just shy of her 13th birthday, my oldest daughter looked at me and said, "Mom, do you know something I realized?"

I braced myself. "What?"

"In five years," she told me, "I'll graduate from high school."

Five. Years.

It hit me like a freight train—so long and yet, compared to the lifespan of my child, breathtakingly short.

Then she hit me with part two.

"You know what else?" she asked.

"Well," I said, "based on what you just told me, I'm not sure I want to know. But lay it on me."

She looked at me, totally serious. "When I graduate from high school and go to college, you'll have a kid in college, a kid in high school, a kid in middle school, *and* a kid in elementary school."

I blinked. She wasn't wrong. She was right. Completely, terrifyingly right.

"And," she added helpfully, "if my math is correct, it'll be that way for *two years.*"

At this point, my brain was reeling. But she wasn't done.

"I don't like it," she said

"Why?" I asked

"Because it makes *me* feel old."

I had to laugh. Because if she feels old at twelve, I have no idea what I'm supposed to feel at forty.

But the thing is—I've never really felt like a grown-up. Yes, I have a job, a mortgage, and a full-blown family. But that inner sense of having arrived at adulthood? Still waiting on that.

Maybe that's part of what raising kids does to you. It keeps you suspended in this odd place between nostalgia and forward motion. Between holding onto their childhood and trying to prepare them for the future. Between remembering your own awkward middle school years and watching them live theirs in real time.

Maybe that's what keeps me on my toes. What keeps me curious. What keeps me honest about how little I actually know.

Maybe my kids are my growth mindset.

Because with them, I'm never quite done. I'm always adjusting. Always learning. Always slightly overwhelmed and wildly in love with the humans they are becoming—and with who I get to become alongside them.

25

The Lesson Behind the Lesson

At some point when my kids were little, my husband and I started teaching them how to *earn back* things they lost after misbehavior. It felt like a good system. Mess up, face a consequence—but also learn that with effort and repair, you can recover.

Hit your sibling? You might lose a half hour of TV, or your tablet, for the afternoon. But help clean up the living room without being asked? Apologize genuinely? Follow through on some age-appropriate accountability? You could earn that time back.

We liked the message: You can mess up *and* grow. Because isn't that how life works? Most of the time, you get a second chance.

But one day, I gave my son a consequence—and without missing a beat, he looked me square in the face and said, "That's okay, Mom. I can just earn it back."

It floored me.

What he was learning wasn't that his behavior needed correction. What he was learning was that there weren't *really* consequences. Because he could always fix it. Later.

And wow—was that a gut check.

It was one of those parenting moments that knocks the wind out of you a little. You think you've been teaching one thing. You feel proud of your approach. And then your kid shows you, clearly and unapologetically, that what they're *actually* internalizing might be something else entirely.

So we regrouped. We didn't throw the whole system away— we still believe in repair, in second chances—but we started being much more intentional about how and when things could be earned back.

Some consequences are final. Just like in real life. And now we're honest and direct with them about it: "If you do this, this will happen. And you won't be able to earn it back."

Because second chances are beautiful—but they don't always come. And part of our job is to help them tell the difference.

V

Rooted and Rising

"Stop saying 'we're pregnant.' You're not pregnant. Do you have to squeeze a watermelon-sized person out of your lady hole? No." – Mila Kunis

26

Dear Moms

This one is for you.

For the ones who spent years growing and feeding other people. For the ones whose bodies have changed and changed again. For the ones who've forgotten what it feels like to belong fully to themselves.

If you've ever stood in front of a mirror and wondered who you are now...

If you've ever tried on jeans or a version of your old self and felt like neither quite fit...

If you're just now learning how to take up space again—not for anyone else, but for *you*...

I see you.

You're still in there. You've always been in there. And maybe now, slowly, you're becoming *you* again.

This isn't about going back. There is no going back—not to our pre-baby bodies, not to our pre-kid lives, not to the versions of ourselves we were before motherhood cracked us open and rebuilt us into something new.

But there is forward. There is softness and strength. There is reclamation. There is the quiet joy of asking yourself: What do *I* want? What feels good to *me*? What would it look like to care for myself—not out of guilt, but out of love?

For many of us, the answer is still forming. Maybe we're just beginning to ask the question. Maybe we're in the messy middle. Maybe we're clawing our way toward something steadier, stretch mark by stretch mark, calendar conflict by calendar conflict.

Wherever you are in the process, this next part is for you.

For the body you live in.

For the person you're becoming.

For the woman still learning how to belong to herself again.

I see you.

27

Reflections on Pregnancy

P regnancy is nothing short of miraculous. Did you know that during those nine months, a person's blood volume increases by nearly 20%? Their body grows an entirely new organ—a placenta—that can weigh close to a pound by the time the baby arrives. Alongside that, there can be up to two pounds of amniotic fluid and an added six to eight pounds of fat stores, all carefully preparing to nurture the tiny human growing inside.

It's awe-inspiring, yes. But it's also hard. Uncomfortable. And sometimes downright messy. Our bodies shift and change almost daily over those ten months (yes, ten), in ways that aren't always pretty or easy to explain.

Beyond the physical transformations, there's another layer many pregnant people have to navigate: the commentary. Friends, family, even strangers can't seem to resist weighing in on how a pregnant body looks or feels. Over four pregnancies, I heard it all—from the bewildered, "Are you sure there's only one in there?" to the blunt, "Whoa! You're huge!" and the ever-popular, "Are you sure your due date is right?"

Here's the truth: if I were to gain 40 pounds without a baby growing inside me, it would be considered rude—and rightly so—to comment on my body. But during pregnancy, those social rules somehow evaporate.

What's a person growing a tiny human to do in the face of this paradox? I often smiled and laughed, even when those comments stung. But no one should have to fake comfort or humor while doing one of the hardest jobs there is.

Pregnancy deserves kindness. It deserves respect. It deserves to be held with gentle eyes, not scrutinized or critiqued.

So, here's a friendly reminder to all the moms out there: it's okay to say no. It's okay to be offended by comments that don't honor your experience. It's okay to gently educate those around you about what growing a human really means. Your boundaries and feelings matter.

And to anyone who hasn't grown a tiny human: if you don't have something kind or supportive to say, the best choice is to say nothing at all. But if you do have a genuine compliment or encouragement, it will mean the world.

Because growing life is one of the most incredible things a body can do—and it deserves to be met with kindness, respect, and love.

28

What No One Told Me About the After

Everything I didn't know about postpartum could fill a book—which is kind of ironic, since now at least some of it is going into one.

I thought I was prepared for the postpartum period. I attended birth class, read the assigned articles, asked the questions, and packed the hospital bag. But a few things still took me completely by surprise.

Like the emptiness.

For forty weeks (that's really ten months, by the way), my body wasn't my own. It was home to a tiny human I was growing. I felt them move. I talked to them. And then one day, they were on the outside.

And everything they shifted on the inside—my muscles, my organs—suddenly felt out of place. My body felt wrong. I felt hollow. Empty.

Physically, it was hard to stand. It was hard to breathe. My very core had shifted. And yet I was expected to go on like nothing had happened.

Not only that, we expect postpartum mothers to host visitors.

To share their baby. To take perfectly posed, beautifully filtered photos. And all the while, we're wearing diapers.

Yes, diapers. That's something newborns and their mamas have in common—matching outfits, if you will. Because the bleeding? It goes on and on. And then on some more, just for good measure.

Throw in the hormonal free fall, and it's a miracle anyone in the household survives.

I'll never forget sitting on the couch with my grandmother after my first child was born. Out of nowhere, I just started sobbing. Big, wet, ugly tears. Snot, too. The whole works.

She handed me a tissue and said calmly, "There, there. Let it out."

"I don't even know why I'm crying," I said, frustrated.

"I know," she said. "And you won't for a while."

That moment lives in me. Because what she offered me wasn't a solution—it was permission. To feel, to fall apart a little, to not know.

We've normalized the postpartum period to the point that we've stopped seeing it. Stopped acknowledging what women are actually going through. However a baby comes into the world, we are torn open by the process and expected to carry on like we're fine. Despite the sleep deprivation. Despite the internal chaos. Despite the diapers and the hormones and the pain.

It's time to be more honest about the beginning.

Not to scare people. But to normalize the need to rest. To be held. To be taken care of. So we don't have to fight for those things later on.

With each of my children, I took more time during this period. I leaned into the quiet, the recovery, the recalibration.

And, ok, I wasn't always very good at it (just ask my husband). But I worked at it and took things slowly because I began to understand that it wasn't just for the baby—it was for me. My body needed it. My spirit needed it. After my second child, it was quite literally medically necessary. But after that, it became something else: *a choice.*

A choice to heal.

A choice to be soft with myself.

A choice to name the beginning for what it truly is—not a blur to rush through, but a sacred threshold.

So here's what I'll say, now that I've lived it:

Give yourself the space.

Ask for what you need.

Let the healing matter.

Because postpartum isn't just the "after." It's the beginning of everything. And you deserve to begin well.

29

Shifting Plans

I always imagined I'd be at least 30 before I started having kids.

I was a high-achieving, high-performing student, determined to channel that drive into a meaningful career. Motherhood was in the plan—but later. Much later.

And then something unexpected happened.

As my husband neared his 30th birthday, he and his friends began talking—not about jobs or travel—but about wanting to become fathers.

Honestly, none of the women in our friend group saw that coming. The men were the ones ready to start families. It was…unexpected.

And suddenly, the math didn't work in my favor. I am two years my husband's junior. There was no way we could both become parents by 30 unless I adjusted my timeline or he adjusted his.

And so we talked.

The more we talked, the more I realized I was open to shifting things. Motherhood was always part of the plan—maybe just not exactly how (or when) I'd envisioned it. Maybe it didn't have to be.

My first child was born while I was still a graduate student. My second arrived after that role turned into a full-time job. And it didn't take long for me to realize that the career path I was on—one I had worked so hard to build—didn't mesh with being the kind of parent I wanted to be.

It was heartbreaking.

I had studied workplace discrimination. I had taught about it. And then I started experiencing it. It's sobering to watch your lived experience mirror the very case studies you once analyzed. So I made a choice—a deliberate, conscious choice—to prioritize my family over my career.

And it stung a little. Not because it was the wrong decision, but because it forced a deep reckoning with the person I thought I was going to become. The version of me I'd spent so many years building toward. I let her go.

But I don't regret it—not for a moment.

In my next job interview, I was clear: I have children. My kids will always come first. "You can replace me," I said, "and I can find another job. But I can't redo motherhood. I only get one shot at that."

It was terrifying, but they must have respected that honesty—they gave me the job. I worked there happily until it no longer fit my family. And then, again, I moved on.

Every opportunity I've accepted since has come with the same caveat: *they come first.*

That doesn't mean I'm invisible. It doesn't mean I've disappeared. Prioritizing them doesn't mean abandoning myself.

Because part of putting them first is modeling what it looks like to be a full human being. I want them to see that I can work hard. That I can say no. That I can have hobbies and friends and boundaries. That I can cheer them on from the sidelines and still go after my own goals. I want them to see me make hard choices—and own them. I want them to know that it's okay not to do everything.

At the end of the day, I'm nothing like the person I thought I would be.

Time will tell whether this version of me is someone I'll always be proud of.

But right now? I think so.

30

Rebuilding

I'll never forget sitting in the urogynecologist's office after an exam. Four kids in, and I had officially become a medical anomaly. My beautiful, wonderful children had torn me open four times—taking with them some of the pieces that made me function.

My body had become so rare that at routine appointments, the doctor would often ask if medical students could observe the exam—because, as she put it, "they may never see anything like this again."

I knew things were unusual. I knew there was damage. But I wasn't prepared for what came next.

"I think it's time we consider a hysterectomy," she said gently, handing me pamphlets I didn't want. I blinked. Then blinked again.

"I'm sorry—what?"

I was 37 years old.

I knew we were done having children (ask me about giving birth at 27 versus 37 sometime—oof), but I hadn't realized that the door would be closed for good. So suddenly. So surgically.

Menopause—well, menopause lets the idea of motherhood, so central to my identity, slip away quietly over time. But this? This was different. This was final. This was general anesthesia and sharp knives.

And I grieved.

The doctor let me cry. She didn't rush me. She didn't minimize the loss. She gave me space to feel the full weight of it.

They needed to use all the ligaments that had once supported my uterus to rebuild the damage caused by years of growing and birthing tiny humans. They stitched me back together— using my own body to do it—but they had to take something from me in the process. A small, miraculous organ that helped me become who I am.

It was heartbreaking. It was a relief. It was everything, all at once.

And the recovery? The recovery was brutal.

Your core is your core for a reason. When it's taken apart and sewn back together, nothing works right. It hurt to move. It hurt to breathe. I went from being a capable, resourceful woman to someone who couldn't walk to the bathroom without help.

(And my bladder didn't work for a while anyway—but that's another story.)

Humility became my closest companion. I couldn't do anything. Anything.

My partner? My family? My village? They held me up— literally. It was the first time in my life that I found myself on the receiving end of a Meal Train. Food appeared at our doorstep, and I was often too medicated or in too much pain to thank the people who brought it.

(To everyone I missed during that time: thank you. Truly.)

Our village isn't huge, but it is mighty. And it carried me through.

So did my partner. So did my kids—shockingly patient, unflinchingly supportive, offering me the space and grace I needed to get through.

I know many women who bounce back quickly after a hysterectomy. I was not one of them.

My surgery wasn't laparoscopic. It wasn't routine. It wasn't just a removal. It was a rebuilding—of my body, yes, but also of myself. And in the weeks and months that followed, I had to rethink who I was. As a woman. As a mother. As a human.

It was physical. It was emotional. And some days, I think I'm still reeling from it.

But I'm also still here.

Still becoming.

31

Becoming Me

When my first daughter was born, I posted online about the feeling of being touched out. Just two weeks into motherhood, I wrote that I never wanted to put her down—and yet somehow, I also needed my own space.

It would take me over a decade to find that space.

In the years that followed, I was rarely alone. Even when I was physically by myself, I wasn't really *by* myself. I was replaying conversations, making mental grocery lists, worrying about developmental milestones, and remembering (OK, mostly forgetting) to move the wet laundry to the dryer before bedtime. I was anticipating needs before they were spoken, meeting them before anyone noticed, and putting my own needs at the bottom of every list.

I still am.

That's the part of motherhood that's hard to explain unless you've lived it—the *unseen* labor. Not just the daily tasks, but the constant emotional load. The vigilance. The preemptive thinking. The way you learn to live on behalf of everyone else.

How sometimes, you forget to live on behalf of yourself.

To be clear, I'm not trying to exclude other people who parent. But I am a mother, and this is my experience.

And in my experience, reclaiming space for myself was not something that just *happened* when the kids got older. I had to fight for it. I had to name it as necessary. I had to personally believe I was worth it—even when I felt guilty for taking it.

But I've more than earned it.

On the verge of my 40th birthday, I had a realization that stopped me in my tracks as I reflected on my motherhood journey: from 2011 through 2024, my body was never fully my own.

Thirteen years. Thirteen years of growing, nurturing, and recovering from making the tiny humans who now fill nearly every waking moment of my life.

But this isn't just about them. It's about me—and (truly) about anyone else out there who's spent years living in service of little ones.

Because practically speaking, those years meant constant change. My body—its shape, weight, and abilities—was always in flux. Pregnancy, postpartum, breastfeeding, weaning, repeat. Add a hysterectomy and a long recovery, and you've got quite the ride.

In 2025, for the first time in thirteen years, I can say: I am neither growing nor feeding another person from my body. I've healed from surgery. For the first time in a long while, I get to decide what to do with this body—just for me.

I'm eating for me. I'm working out for me. It feels deliciously selfish. Indulgent, even. And deeply necessary.

Of course, life has its sense of humor. Just as I'm reclaiming my body, it's shifting again.

Perimenopause has entered the chat, and let me tell you, she's got some opinions. My hormones ride an unpredictable roller coaster. Sleep is unreliable. My moods swing like a metronome. The body that once responded to a few days of clean eating or a good workout now just... shrugs. And the brain fog? It's real. Some days, I barely know my own name.

It feels a little unfair, honestly. After all that time spent growing other people, I thought I'd get a few years of steady ground to grow back into myself.

But maybe this is just another kind of growth—not a return to the person I was before motherhood, but a recalibration. A renegotiation. A reminder that I get to keep evolving.

So here I am, owning this body, this phase, this version of me—at least a little, between my shifts as an unpaid Uber driver and family scheduler.

And honestly? That seems like a pretty good gift to give myself.

And guess what? My kids tell me I'm a happier person. And they're right.

So cheers to all the mamas and people who've grown tiny humans and who are still riding this wild, hormonal roller coaster.

I see you.

You've got this.

VI

Epilogue

"I don't know what's more exhausting about parenting: the getting up early, or acting like you know what you're doing." – Jim Gaffigan

32

One Messy, Beautiful Day At A Time

On the day your child came to you, in whatever form, you grew up.

Maybe not all at once. Maybe not in a way you could explain, but something shifted. You became responsible for a life that wasn't your own—and from that day forward, everything changed.

You started showing up in ways no one could have prepared you for. You held things together when it would've been easier to walk away. You stayed up late to finish the laundry, pack lunches, or build science fair display boards. You woke early to comfort a child who needed nothing but you. You found patience you didn't know you had—and sometimes you didn't. You lost your temper. You apologized. You kept going anyway.

There are so many moments that no one sees. The little ones, the hard ones, the beautiful ones. You are in all of them.

There's a myth out there that parenting is about shaping children. But more and more, I believe parenting is about being shaped by them. It's about becoming someone softer, stronger, more honest. Someone who knows how to say *I'm sorry.* Someone who's learning to let go, even while holding tight. Someone who is stretched, grown, undone, and rebuilt—again and again.

This is for you. For the days when you're wondering if you're getting any of it right. For the moments when everything feels like too much. For the nights when you want to quit—but don't.

This is for the parents who are still showing up, one messy, beautiful day at a time.

If no one has told you lately, you're doing an incredible job. Not a perfect job. But an incredible one.

You are the steady hum beneath your child's wild, brilliant life. You are the rhythm they come back to, the home they return to, the love that doesn't ask to be earned.

You are enough.

And thank you, sincerely, for reading this.

Author's Note

To my husband—thank you for quietly (and sometimes not so quietly) holding us all together. For your steady support, your dad jokes, your funny shorts, and your willingness to laugh at life's chaos right alongside me. You are my calm in the storm and the reason we all know how to laugh through it.

To my children—these stories would not exist without you. Literally. Every one of you made me a mother in a different way. You gave me material, yes, but you also gave me meaning. Thank you for stretching my heart, my time, and my capacity in ways I never imagined. I love each of you more than sleep, which is saying something.

To our village—to our family and our friends—thank you. For the meals, the text check-ins, the Trader Joe runs, the late-night venting sessions, the childcare swaps, and the reminders that none of us are doing this alone. I've felt held. I hope you know you are too.

And to you, the reader—thank you. I can't believe you made it all the way through this collection. Whether you read one story or all of them, whether you laughed, cried, nodded in recognition, or just silently endured it… thank you. It's an honor to be heard.

www.ingramcontent.com/pod-product-compliance
Lightning Source LLC
Chambersburg PA
CBHW070344130626

46556CB00007B/3021